Monster

The Ed Gein Story-Inside the Mind of America's Most Notorious Killer

Elara M. Vintrow

Copyright

All rights reserved. No part of this book may be reproduced, stored in a retrieval system, or transmitted in any form or by any means, electronic, mechanical, photocopying, recording, or otherwise, without the prior written permission of the publisher, except for brief quotations used in reviews.

This book is a work of nonfiction. Any similarity to real persons, living or dead, is coincidental and not intended by the author.

© 2025 by Elara M. Vintrow

Disclaimer

Monster: The Ed Gein Story — Inside the Mind of America's Most Notorious Killer is a work of nonfiction that explores the life, crimes, and psychological profile of Ed Gein, one of the most infamous figures in American criminal history. The content of this book is intended for mature readers and includes discussions of graphic violence, psychological trauma, and other sensitive subjects. While all efforts have been made to present factual and accurate information, the narrative is written with the intention of providing insight into the disturbing nature of Gein's actions and the cultural impact of his crimes.

The descriptions of Ed Gein's life and crimes, including his mental state, motivations, and the repercussions of his actions, are presented based on historical records, interviews, and psychological analyses. However, due to the complexities of mental health and human behavior, some interpretations and conclusions presented may be subjective and speculative in nature.

The names of individuals, places, and events discussed in this book have been carefully included based on their relevance to the story and historical accuracy. However, any resemblance to other real-life individuals, events, or organizations is purely coincidental, unless otherwise noted.

This book is not intended to glorify violence or criminal behavior. It is written to explore the factors that contributed to one of the most disturbing cases of human depravity, while aiming to provide an understanding of the psychological, cultural, and societal forces that shaped Ed Gein's life and actions. Reader discretion is strongly advised.

Table of Contents

Introduction	8
Chapter One	19
The Origins of a Monster	19
Chapter Two	**28**
The Small-Town Setting	28
Chapter Three	37
The Loss of a Mother	37
Chapter Four	**47**
The Dark Descent Begins	47
Chapter Five	**57**
The Horror Unveiled	57
Chapter Six	68
Behind the Masks	68
Chapter Seven	78
The Psychological Profile of Ed Gein	78
Chapter Eight	**88**
Gein's Gruesome Hobby	88
Chapter Nine	**98**
The Police Investigation	98
Chapter Ten	**108**
The Trial of Ed Gein	108
Chapter Eleven	**118**
The Aftermath and Cultural Impact	118
Chapter Twelve	**128**
The Legacy of a Monster	128

Introduction

"A monster is made, not born."

This chilling truth resonates through the story of Ed Gein, one of the most infamous figures in American criminal history. His name became synonymous with grotesque acts of violence and morbid obsession, forever embedded in the collective consciousness of society. But how did this quiet, introverted man from the rural town of Plainfield, Wisconsin, become the monster that inspired some of the most terrifying characters in horror fiction?

Ed Gein's story raises difficult questions about the nature of evil and the forces that shape it. Was he born with a predisposition for violence, or did his environment and upbringing play a pivotal role in creating the man who would become known as "The Butcher of Plainfield"? In the case of Ed Gein, the answer may lie somewhere between the two—an intricate blend of nature and nurture that combined to create a tragic figure whose horrific actions left an indelible mark on American culture.

Ed Gein's early life was defined by isolation, deprivation, and an overbearing mother. Born on August 27, 1906, to George and Augusta Gein, Ed's childhood was far from typical. His father was an alcoholic who barely provided for the family, while his mother, Augusta, was a devout, domineering woman who kept a tight grip on her sons. Augusta was a firm believer in her own religious zealotry, raising her children with an oppressive and judgmental attitude. She taught them that all women were inherently evil and that men should avoid the temptations of the opposite sex. Augusta's influence was all-encompassing—Ed's interactions with others were limited, his social skills stunted, and his ability to form healthy relationships was suffocated by his mother's control.

Ed's brother, Henry, was the more independent of the two boys, often taking on manual labor jobs and helping with the farm work. However, in 1944, Henry died in a mysterious fire while out on a brush-clearing mission with Ed. The death was ruled accidental, but it added to Ed's growing sense of loneliness and abandonment. His relationship with his mother became even more intense after Henry's death, with Ed becoming increasingly devoted to Augusta, following her every command. In a sense, she was the only constant in his life, and her belief in his role as a devoted son would have a lasting impact on his psyche.

Ed's early life was also marked by extreme poverty, which further isolated him from society. The Geins lived on a dilapidated farm on the outskirts of Plainfield, a small town in Wisconsin. The property was run-down and isolated, offering no opportunities for social interaction outside of school. Ed attended school sporadically, often becoming the target of teasing and bullying from his classmates. The harsh rural environment only deepened Ed's sense of alienation and powerlessness, and his desperate need for validation would later manifest in the twisted ways that he sought to assert control over his life.

As Ed grew older, he became more withdrawn, spending his days working on the farm and occasionally taking odd jobs in town. His social interactions were limited, and he became known for his strange behavior. He was often seen as an oddball, the kind of person people talked about but avoided. While the town of Plainfield seemed to ignore him, the seeds of Ed's future crimes were being sown in the isolation and psychological turmoil that marked his early life.

The turning point came in 1945, when Augusta Gein passed away. Ed's world crumbled. His mother had been the center of his existence, and her death left him utterly unmoored. For a brief period, Ed seemed to be freed from her domineering presence, but the trauma of her influence lingered. It was around this time that

Ed began his descent into madness. His grief and obsession with his mother's memory became more pronounced, leading him to commit a series of increasingly disturbing acts.

Ed's crimes began small—digging up graves in local cemeteries to steal corpses. He believed that by exhuming the dead, he could "recreate" his mother, who he still saw as the only source of comfort in his life. These grave robbing excursions were a manifestation of his obsession with death and control, a desperate attempt to connect with the mother he had lost, but in the most grotesque way imaginable. Over time, his actions grew more depraved. He began using the body parts he stole from the graves to create items in his house—masks made from human skin, lampshades from human flesh, and a complete "female suit" crafted from the bodies of his victims. Each creation reflected a twisted desire to embody the women he was so terrified of and obsessed with, particularly the domineering, puritanical figure of his mother.

But Ed's crimes didn't remain limited to grave robbing. In 1954, he committed his first known murder: a tavern owner named Mary Hogan. Hogan's disappearance would later be linked to Gein, but at the time, the police were baffled by her sudden vanishing. Ed's second murder occurred in 1957, when he killed Bernice Worden, a local hardware store owner. It was her death that finally led to Ed's arrest. After Bernice's disappearance, the police traced her last known customer to Ed Gein's property.

When they searched his home, they discovered the horrors that lay hidden behind its walls.

The discovery of Gein's crimes shocked the nation. Inside his house, investigators found human remains scattered throughout the property—decapitated heads, skin sewn into clothing, and jars filled with body parts. The grotesque nature of Gein's collection sent shockwaves across the United States, and his name became synonymous with horror. The media frenzy surrounding the case turned Ed Gein into a symbol of depravity and madness, one that would influence generations of filmmakers and writers.

The significance of Ed Gein's story extends far beyond his gruesome acts. His crimes left an indelible mark on American history and culture, particularly in the realm of horror. Gein's grotesque creations and morbid obsessions inspired some of the most iconic figures in the genre, including Norman Bates in *Psycho*, Leatherface in *The Texas Chainsaw Massacre*, and Buffalo Bill in *The Silence of the Lambs*. These characters, born from the nightmare of Gein's actions, would go on to define horror for decades. The archetype of the "madman" who lives in isolation, creating monstrous works of art from the bodies of his victims, became a staple of horror fiction, and Gein's legacy lived on in the works of filmmakers like Alfred Hitchcock, Tobe Hooper, and Jonathan Demme.

In many ways, Gein's story raised profound questions about the nature of evil. Was he born a monster, or was he shaped by his environment? The answer is undoubtedly complex. While Gein's early life and upbringing played a significant role in his development, his descent into madness was also the result of a unique combination of psychological instability, emotional trauma, and external influences. Ed Gein did not simply wake up one day as a killer; his environment, his upbringing, and his mental state combined to create the perfect storm of violence and depravity.

Gein's story is a haunting reminder of the dark corners of the human psyche. It forces us to confront uncomfortable truths about the power of isolation, the impact of trauma, and the potential for evil within each of us. His crimes, once uncovered, revealed a deeper horror than mere murder—it was a reflection of a man whose entire existence was consumed by an obsession with death, with control, and with an impossible attempt to recreate the past. The legacy of Ed Gein lives on, not just in the twisted horror films he inspired, but in the chilling reminder that monsters are not born—they are made.

Through the lens of Gein's life and crimes, we are forced to reckon with the uncomfortable reality that sometimes, evil is not an external force but something that can be cultivated within the darkest recesses of the human soul.

Chapter One

The Origins of a Monster

"Monsters are real, and ghosts are too. They live inside of us, and sometimes, they win." – Stephen King

Ed Gein was born on August 27, 1906, in La Crosse, Wisconsin, though it was Plainfield, a small, sleepy town in central Wisconsin, where his story would be etched in the annals of horror. The town itself, with its sparse population and rustic charm, seemed a world apart from the darkness that would unfold in the life of one of America's most infamous criminals. But it was in this rural setting that Gein's tale would unfold, a tale that would horrify the world for decades to come.

Ed's parents, George and Augusta Gein, were the cornerstone of his troubled beginnings. George, a heavy drinker, worked sporadically as a farmer and had little to no influence on his son's life. His presence, though physically present in their home, was marked more by absence in terms of emotional or psychological support. Ed's mother, Augusta, however, was the central, domineering force in his life. She was a woman of rigid beliefs, devoutly religious, and deeply puritanical in her views about the world. Her influence on Ed was suffocating, and it is here that the roots of his later madness can be traced.

Augusta was not just a mother; she was a god-like figure in Ed's eyes. She preached daily about the evils of the world, particularly the sins of women and the dangers of sexuality. According to her, all women were corrupt, responsible for the downfall of mankind. She would often tell Ed that men were weak, easily led astray by their desires, while women were instruments of evil, enticing men to sin. She instilled in him an intense, almost pathological, fear of women and a deep sense of guilt over any desire or attraction he might feel towards them.

In many ways, Augusta's religious extremism was her method of controlling Ed. She kept him isolated from the outside world, sheltering him from the typical joys of childhood. Ed's social interactions were few and far between, his only refuge being the home and the teachings of his mother. His childhood was marked by loneliness and a sense of being trapped under the oppressive weight of his mother's beliefs. Augusta taught Ed to distrust others, particularly women, and to view the world as a place full of sin and damnation. She even kept him from attending school regularly, a move that would isolate him further from his peers and entrench his world view as shaped by her.

As Ed grew older, Augusta's control only intensified. She prevented him from developing any relationships with girls or women, forbidding him from dating and socializing. She isolated him further from the outside world, reinforcing his belief that the only acceptable woman was one who was pure, chaste, and under her complete control. She created a world where Ed's needs were secondary to her own, where his identity was shaped solely by her warped worldview.

The impact of Augusta's overbearing presence on Ed's mental state was profound. As a young boy, Ed had begun to show signs of the psychological distress that would manifest in his later life. He had few friends and often found solace in the company of animals, particularly his pets. His relationship with his mother grew increasingly dysfunctional as he reached adolescence. While most boys his age began to develop an interest in girls, Ed remained entirely under Augusta's control, his every thought and desire dictated by her influence.

The Gein household itself was as bleak as the family dynamics that shaped it. The family's farm, located just outside of Plainfield, was dilapidated and isolated. Ed and his mother lived in a run-down house that was sparsely furnished, a place devoid of warmth or comfort. The house, much like Ed's life, was filled with the remnants of a once-prosperous existence, a place that had long since fallen into neglect. The farm was a reflection of Augusta's own rigid control over their lives—an environment of neglect, deprivation, and isolation. Ed's life was one of stifling routine, where his only purpose was to serve his mother and uphold the narrow, restrictive worldview she imposed upon him.

By the time Ed reached his teenage years, his psyche had become increasingly disturbed. His mother's influence, combined with his deep isolation, left Ed unable to form meaningful relationships with others. He was a social outcast, a figure of ridicule among his peers, but in his mind, it was his mother's teachings that were the truth. He was a lonely boy, but one who was fiercely loyal to his mother's teachings, even as they became more out of touch with reality. His desire for affection and connection was buried under layers of shame and guilt, leaving him with no avenue for emotional expression.

In the years that followed, Ed's mental state deteriorated further. The more he clung to the twisted teachings of his mother, the more disconnected he became from the world around him. By the time he entered adulthood, Ed's mind had become a labyrinth of confusion, a place where the line between reality and delusion was blurred. Augusta's death in 1945 would be the catalyst for the tragic events that would unfold in Ed's life, but the seeds of his monstrous actions were planted long before that. The suffocating grip of his mother's influence on Ed's psyche was unshakable, and it would lead him down a path that would ultimately redefine the concept of horror in America.

The formative years of Ed Gein's life were marked by isolation, deprivation, and an unrelenting sense of guilt. His mother's religious extremism and the suffocating control she exercised over him created a toxic environment that stunted his emotional development and warped his perception of the world. In many ways, Augusta's twisted teachings served as the foundation for the horrors that would later unfold in Ed's life. The foundation of a monster was built in the most unlikely of places: a small, rural town, a decaying farm, and the cruel grip of a mother's love.

Chapter Two

The Small-Town Setting

"Plainfield was a quiet town, a place where neighbors waved to each other in passing, and secrets were rare—at least, that's what people believed. But for one man, Plainfield became the perfect sanctuary for his dark, twisted fantasies. In this small corner of Wisconsin, Ed Gein hid in plain sight, his horrendous acts masked by the very qualities that made the town so tight-knit."

Plainfield, Wisconsin, was the kind of town where life moved at a slow pace, a place where everyone knew everyone, or at least thought they did. Its small population and rural setting painted the picture of a peaceful, idyllic life. Yet beneath the surface of this seemingly quaint, tight-knit community, a darkness thrived that no one could have imagined. Plainfield's culture of privacy, self-sufficiency, and social conformity made it the perfect environment for someone like Ed Gein to carry out his gruesome crimes without raising suspicion.

The town itself was modest, with a population that hovered around 1,000 residents in the 1950s and 1960s, many of whom were farmers, shopkeepers, and other working-class folk. Life in Plainfield was simple, marked by the rhythms of nature and the cycles of the farming year. It was a place where people valued their privacy, not because they had anything to hide, but because that was the way life was. The small-town values of the Midwest dictated that everyone should keep to themselves, with little need for outsiders to probe into one another's business. This atmosphere of quiet routine, where every corner of the town seemed familiar and every house was easily identifiable, provided Ed Gein with a unique camouflage for his criminal activities.

For much of Ed's life, he was seen as a benign, oddball figure, someone who stuck to himself and lived on the outskirts of the town's main social circles. He wasn't a criminal in anyone's eyes, but rather a reclusive, strange man who kept to his mother's house, rarely venturing far from it. He didn't fit the mold of the typical small-town man, but in the close-knit society of Plainfield, this didn't draw as much attention as it might have elsewhere. The townspeople, many of whom were busy with their own lives, simply wrote him off as an eccentric bachelor living under the thumb of his overbearing mother, Augusta Gein. It was the 1940s and 1950s, a time when small towns prided themselves on being insular and close-knit, and in such an environment, strangeness was often tolerated as long as it didn't disrupt the status quo.

Ed's life was a series of routines. He worked as a handyman, often taking small jobs for neighbors, but never getting too involved in any of the social events or gatherings that the town was known for. He was known to frequent the local tavern, where he would sit in silence, rarely engaging in conversation, a quiet observer rather than an active participant. Though people saw him around, there was little curiosity about his life. It wasn't uncommon in rural towns for people to be left to their own devices, as long as they weren't openly disruptive. Ed was merely a fixture, his oddities being part of the town's patchwork.

In a town like Plainfield, where everyone had their own lives to lead and socializing was mostly reserved for gatherings at the local church or the few neighborhood events, there was little room for questions about the man who lived with his mother on the outskirts. The truth is, the small-town atmosphere that Plainfield thrived on was one of benign neglect. People respected each other's privacy, and that respect extended to Ed Gein. It was a pattern that allowed him to flourish in the shadows of the community, without any of the intrusive oversight that larger cities might have provided.

However, this sense of community and respect for privacy came at a cost. In Plainfield, everyone respected each other's space, but this created an environment where secrets could fester. The community's deep-seated belief in privacy and social conformity meant that it was easy for Ed to keep his own life sealed off from the rest of the town. Despite his reclusive nature and unusual behaviors, no one asked questions. No one felt it was their place to probe into Ed's life, particularly when his behaviors didn't seem outwardly harmful. His oddities were passed off as the eccentricities of a man who had never quite adjusted to the rhythms of adult life. The reality, though, was that Ed Gein's criminal activities were taking root in the very heart of Plainfield, and no one suspected a thing.

It wasn't just Ed's oddities that went unnoticed; his living conditions were equally neglected by those who passed by his home. His farmhouse, situated just outside of town, had become the setting for some of the most macabre activities in American criminal history, yet it remained largely untouched by the curiosity of neighbors. The house, like Ed himself, was isolated—cut off by overgrown vegetation and a distance that served as a physical barrier between the house and the rest of Plainfield. Those who occasionally passed by the Gein property saw little that was out of the ordinary. The home was rundown, the lawn untended, but this was hardly unusual for a small town where many families lived on farms that were slowly being abandoned in favor of more industrialized methods of living.

Ed's mother, Augusta, had passed away in 1945, but Ed continued to live in the house for years afterward, holding on to her memory in the only way he knew how. By the time he began committing his crimes, Ed was increasingly isolated, withdrawing more and more from the world around him. He became obsessed with death, with the human body, and with recreating his mother's image. But all of this was hidden behind a mask of normalcy—a man doing odd jobs, paying for his groceries with a small pension, keeping to himself in a small, quiet town.

The townspeople continued with their lives, blissfully unaware of the horrors occurring so close to them. Their preoccupation with maintaining privacy, their unwillingness to intrude upon one another's lives, meant that Ed's darkest secrets were well hidden. Even when Ed would sometimes take small jobs for his neighbors, his behavior never seemed out of place enough to warrant suspicion. A few odd interactions—an awkward smile, a stiff posture—were dismissed as the quirks of a man who had been alone for far too long.

The Gein family farmhouse, once a home to Ed and his domineering mother, had become a tomb of sorts. To anyone driving by, the house seemed like any other house in the countryside—weathered, worn, and slightly decrepit. People, including the occasional visiting lawman, would have seen no reason to think there was something nefarious about it. In a town so focused on maintaining a facade of quiet order, Ed's private life, and the horror it contained, was simply beyond the purview of those around him. The very things that should have raised red flags—his lack of social engagement, his eccentricities, his increasingly erratic behavior—were accepted as part of life in Plainfield.

The tight-knit, private nature of Plainfield made it the perfect hiding place for Ed Gein. In a town where secrets were buried under layers of routine and respect for one another's boundaries, Ed's dark secrets remained untouched, like weeds growing in a neglected garden, unnoticed until it was far too late. The very privacy that protected him ultimately enabled his descent into madness, allowing him to commit acts so vile that they would eventually redefine the world's understanding of horror and criminality.

Chapter Three

The Loss of a Mother

"A mother's love is endless," they say, but for Ed Gein, the love he had for his mother was twisted and unyielding, even in death.

Augusta Gein's death in 1945 was not just the loss of a mother for Ed—it was the shattering of the only world he had ever known. She had been the center of his existence for as long as he could remember, her influence over him profound and absolute. Her death marked the beginning of Ed's descent into madness, a spiraling decline that led him to commit some of the most horrific crimes in American history. To understand the role Augusta's death played in Ed's transformation, it's crucial to first examine the tightly woven relationship between them—a bond that was suffocating, domineering, and, ultimately, destructive.

Ed Gein was born in 1906 to Augusta and George Gein in Plainfield, Wisconsin. While George was a mild-mannered alcoholic who worked sporadically, Augusta was a deeply religious and controlling woman who dominated the household. From an early age, Ed was conditioned to see women as inherently sinful and corrupt, a perspective Augusta instilled in him with her strict, unyielding beliefs. She saw herself as the sole moral authority in Ed's life, instilling in him a devotion that veered dangerously close to obsession. His world was small and solitary—confined to the farm and shaped entirely by Augusta's presence and guidance.

As Ed grew older, his dependence on his mother only deepened. Augusta isolated him from the outside world, making it clear that any attachment to others, particularly women, was sinful. This deep attachment to his mother left Ed emotionally stunted and incapable of forming healthy relationships with others. Augusta's domination over Ed continued throughout his adult life, even as he reached middle age. She became the focal point of his existence, and his perception of the world was filtered through her dictatorial lens.

When Augusta passed away in December 1945, Ed was left adrift in a world without his only anchor. The loss was catastrophic for him, as it represented not just the death of his mother but the disintegration of the rigid world she had imposed upon him. Her death stripped Ed of the only authority he had ever known and left him in an emotional freefall. His grief was unlike that of any other son. For Ed, his mother's death was not a natural part of life, but an apocalyptic event that left him utterly unmoored. The psychological fallout from this loss was devastating, and it set the stage for the horrors that would soon unfold.

Ed's descent into madness following his mother's death was swift and profound. His emotional breakdown took a darker turn when he began to reject the reality of her passing. Unable to cope with the finality of her death, Ed's delusions began to take root. He started to live in denial of her absence, attempting to preserve her memory by any means necessary. For months after her death, Ed maintained a morbid fixation on Augusta, even going so far as to exhume her body from the local cemetery. It was a desperate attempt to preserve what remained of her, to keep her with him in some form.

On the night of December 8, 1957, Ed entered the Plainfield Cemetery and, using a shovel, dug up his mother's grave. What he found in the freshly disturbed soil, in the cold and damp earth, was not just the remains of the woman who had been his entire world but the reality of his own disintegration. He took her body back to his home, where he proceeded to remove the corpse's skin, which he later tanned, along with other parts of the body. These grisly actions were Ed's attempt to "bring his mother back" in a twisted, macabre sense. In his mind, he was not desecrating her; he was preserving her. It was the only way he could reconcile his feelings of abandonment. His need to keep her alive went beyond the grave—he could not bear the thought of letting her go.

Ed's attempts to preserve Augusta's memory and keep her alive after her death were not limited to the exhumation of her body. He became fixated on the idea of recreating her physical form. In the years following her death, he began creating a grotesque and surreal tribute to his mother—constructing masks, furniture, and even a "female suit" made from human skin. These objects were not just morbid keepsakes, but representations of Ed's attempt to reclaim control over the loss of the one person who had dictated the terms of his life. He sought to transform himself into a woman, perhaps in an effort to reconnect with Augusta's rigid, controlling nature.

The psychological breakdown Ed suffered after his mother's death was not just about loss—it was a desperate attempt to maintain a connection to the only reality he had ever known. His fixation on creating a female form from human remains was his distorted way of preserving the essence of his mother. In the quiet of his home, surrounded by the eerie trophies he had crafted, Ed tried to fill the void left by her passing. The act of cutting, stitching, and crafting the masks was a form of rebirth for

Ed—one that allowed him to feel in control of a world that had shattered around him.

But this need to preserve his mother's memory was not just a psychological mechanism—it was an indication of the profound damage done to Ed's mental state. His isolation grew more extreme as he spent long hours alone with his macabre creations. The line between reality and fantasy blurred in Ed's mind as he began to view the corpses of other women as vessels for his twisted need to recreate the maternal figure he had lost. The women he targeted were not just victims in a series of gruesome murders—they were stand-ins for Augusta. In his mind, he was not killing them for the sake of violence, but for the sake of preserving their bodies as remnants of the mother he could never forget.

As Ed spiraled deeper into delusion, his acts of violence became more brazen and disturbingly ritualistic. He would dig up graves, rob corpses, and desecrate their remains, all in an attempt to hold onto the idea of a woman who had long since passed. In his warped reality, Ed Gein was still a dutiful son—a son who would do whatever it took to keep his mother with him, even if it meant going to unspeakable lengths.

Ed's psychological breakdown, triggered by his mother's death, was compounded by the fact that he never allowed himself to grieve in a healthy way. Augusta had taught him that emotions were to be suppressed, and so he buried his grief deep within himself. Instead of confronting his sorrow, Ed chose to distort it into something darker, into an obsession that would consume him. His isolation, compounded by his delusions, ensured that no one could see the unraveling of his mind until it was too late.

Ed Gein's life after Augusta's death was defined by his attempts to hold on to her memory in ways that were grotesque, delusional, and deeply disturbing. What was once a deeply connected mother-son bond became an unhealthy obsession—a descent into madness that led to the creation of one of the most infamous criminals in American history. Augusta Gein's death was the catalyst, but it was Ed's inability to let go, to accept the finality of death, that turned his grief into something monstrous. The line between love and obsession blurred in Ed's mind, and the result was a tragic, horrifying legacy that would live on in the annals of criminal history.

Ed Gein never truly recovered from the loss of his mother. His attempts to preserve her memory—through exhumation, mutilation, and the construction of grotesque relics—were symptomatic of a man who had no other way to cope with the reality of his mother's death. The psychological damage done to Ed by his mother's death was irreversible. It set him on a path that led to the horrific crimes he would eventually commit, crimes that would make his name synonymous with the darkest corners of human depravity.

In the end, Ed Gein's relationship with his mother—one that had been so controlling, so stifling—would lead to his complete undoing. Her death was not just the loss of a parent; it was the unraveling of a fragile psyche that had been held together by the illusion of control. The monster that Ed Gein became was not born in a vacuum—it was a product of his twisted devotion to a mother who had shaped him into something far beyond human.

Chapter Four

The Dark Descent Begins

The quiet town of Plainfield, Wisconsin, had always been known for its peacefulness, a place where neighbors trusted one another, and life moved at a deliberate, almost predictable pace. Yet behind its serene facade, there lurked a darkness that would later become one of the most infamous cases in American criminal history. Ed Gein, a man who seemed almost invisible in his rural surroundings, would quietly slip into the annals of infamy, not for anything grand or audacious, but for the quiet horrors he unleashed on the small world around him. His criminal activities did not burst forth in violent, chaotic fashion, but were instead gradual, methodical, and deeply unsettling.

In the beginning, Ed's crimes appeared more as extensions of his twisted obsessions than overtly violent actions. His first criminal acts were rooted in a growing fascination with death and the macabre, spurred in part by the domineering presence of his mother, Augusta. While she was alive, she had instilled in him a rigid moral code that combined severe religious dogma with a distorted understanding of purity and sin. She had conditioned him to believe that the world outside their home was a place of corruption, a place he could not trust or be a part of. She was his whole world—her death, in 1945, set the stage for Ed's gradual descent into madness.

Initially, the first crimes were not the murders that would later shock the nation, but rather the theft of body parts from local graveyards. It began innocuously enough. Ed, then in his mid-forties, had already begun to distance himself from the town's people. He spent his days alone on his family's farm, tinkering in his workshop, and focusing on odd, morbid projects. He began visiting local cemeteries, digging up recently buried bodies under the cover of darkness. His motivation, as he would later explain in interviews, was an obsession with the idea of resurrecting his mother. He would exhume the bodies of women who resembled her—blonde, large-framed, and possessing certain physical traits that mirrored Augusta's—hoping to create a life-sized "female suit" that would allow him to step into his mother's role, or at least bring her back in some twisted form.

Ed's reasoning, although deeply disordered, was rooted in the emotional trauma of his childhood. He had been unable to reconcile his need for maternal affection with his mother's unyielding control over him. Augusta's death left him in a vacuum of grief and confusion, and it was this emotional void that led him to increasingly irrational and dangerous actions. In his mind, the women he exhumed were vessels for his mother's resurrection, as though he could piece together the pieces of his lost connection to her. His actions were not those of a man seeking thrill or even destruction. They were, in Ed's mind, the pursuit of a twisted form of redemption—an attempt to reconnect with the only person who had ever truly been a part of his life.

This was where the rationalization of his crimes began. Ed's view of the world had become so warped, so filtered through his years of isolation and dependence on his mother's teachings, that he genuinely believed he was doing no wrong. In his eyes, exhuming the bodies was not a crime but a desperate attempt to create the only bond he had known in his adult life. The psychological factors behind his actions lay in the suppression of his emotional needs, particularly the longing for a maternal connection. Without the comfort of his mother, Ed sought to fill the gap with physical representations of her, namely the corpses of women who he thought embodied the ideal image of motherhood.

As Ed's criminal activities escalated, so too did the horror of his actions. He began not only to exhume bodies but to take them back to his farm, where he meticulously dissected and preserved the remains. At first, he would remove certain parts of the body—hands, faces, and pieces of flesh—and preserve them in jars. But soon, this macabre collection expanded into the construction of masks made from human skin, which he fashioned into grotesque and disturbing suits that he would wear around his property. This marked a significant shift in Ed's psychological state, from a man driven by grief and twisted longing to one driven by an increasingly erratic and violent impulse. He began to create these gruesome trophies not just for a sense of closeness to his mother but also as a way of satisfying his growing need for control. The process of dissecting and creating these objects gave him a semblance of power, a feeling of mastery over life and death.

This obsession with control was amplified by Ed's profound sense of isolation. Without the presence of his mother, and cut off from any meaningful relationships with others, he was left to his own devices. His psychological struggles, compounded by a lack of any support system, took their toll on his mental stability. It's widely believed that Ed suffered from severe schizophrenia, a condition that led him to believe that his actions were justified, even necessary. Schizophrenia, marked by hallucinations, delusions, and disorganized thinking, could explain many of Ed's rationalizations. He was not simply a man trying to satisfy a perverse urge; he was a man who, in his mind, was fulfilling a mission—a mission to resurrect his mother and create a new life for himself in her image.

The psychological factors that contributed to his violent outbursts were a mixture of trauma, isolation, and mental illness. Ed had never learned how to deal with grief, loss, or his emotions in any healthy way. Instead, he internalized these emotions until they manifested in violence. The most disturbing aspect of his psychological state was how he compartmentalized his actions. He never viewed his crimes as anything more than attempts to fill a deep void within himself. He wasn't a monster, as the world would come to call him. In his own mind, he was merely completing a task that needed to be done, like a carpenter constructing a chair or a farmer tilling the soil. This detachment from the gravity of his actions, coupled with his deteriorating mental health, was what allowed him to commit the unimaginable without remorse or recognition of the harm he caused.

Ed's first murders did not come immediately after his exhumations. Instead, they occurred as part of a slow escalation. After several years of body-snatching, Ed's crimes shifted from grave robbing to killing. The first victim, Mary Hogan, was a tavern owner in Plainfield, whom Ed murdered in 1954. He shot her in the face before bringing her body back to his farm. From there, he dissected her and took her face, which he later used as one of his grotesque masks. The second murder, that of Bernice Worden in 1957, followed a similar pattern. After killing her, he removed her organs and hung her body in a shed, almost as if she were another specimen in his grotesque collection.

These murders marked a new phase in Ed's criminal activities. No longer simply content with digging up bodies, he began to kill, to ensure he had access to the fresh remains he needed for his disturbing work. Each murder was an extension of his psychological need for control and connection. Ed rationalized these murders, just as he had with his earlier crimes, through his warped lens of grief and desire. He saw the women he killed not as victims, but as part of his need to rebuild the mother he had lost. They were pieces in a puzzle he had spent his entire adult life trying to complete.

The early stages of Ed Gein's descent into criminality were marked by a blend of psychological trauma, emotional isolation, and a growing obsession with death and control. He rationalized his actions through a lens distorted by his upbringing and mental illness, and his crimes, though horrific, were to him a tragic necessity. As his violent outbursts escalated, so too did the macabre creations he built from human remains, leading him down a path from body snatcher to murderer, all the while justifying his actions through delusions that kept him blind to the immense horror of his crimes.

Chapter Five

The Horror Unveiled

"The human mind is capable of anything—because everything is in it, all the past as well as all the future." — Joseph Conrad

The quiet town of Plainfield, Wisconsin, once a peaceful rural community, became the scene of one of the most grotesque discoveries in American criminal history. On November 16, 1957, the discovery of a missing woman, Bernice Worden, led law enforcement officials to a farmhouse that would reveal horrors beyond belief. What they uncovered inside Ed Gein's home was far more than they could have imagined—a world of human remains, bizarre trophies, and a twisted reality that sent shockwaves through the nation.

The case began with the disappearance of Bernice Worden, the town's beloved hardware store owner. When her son, Frank Worden, entered the store on that fateful morning, he found a trail of blood leading outside, and his mother was nowhere to be found. Her car was missing, but there was no sign of a struggle. It wasn't until the investigation led authorities to Ed Gein's farmhouse that the dark truth began to emerge. Authorities had no idea what they were about to find when they knocked on the door of his seemingly quiet, modest home, located on the outskirts of Plainfield.

When deputies arrived at Gein's farmstead, they were unaware of the true nature of the man who had lived there for so many years, tucked away in isolation with his strange behavior and reclusive lifestyle. As they entered the house, they were immediately struck by a sense of unease. The house, unlike any other, seemed almost frozen in time. It was cold and dark, dimly lit by flickering bulbs. The air carried an unmistakable stench, one that sent chills down the spines of the officers as they stepped into the living room.

The initial discovery was a body—Bernice Worden's body. She had been hung upside down from the rafters, her body disemboweled in the most gruesome manner, with her organs removed and discarded. Her body was mutilated, but it was what was found around her that would send the investigation into a chilling new direction. She wasn't the only victim.

As the authorities scoured the home, they uncovered an arsenal of macabre trophies that defied comprehension. The walls of the house were adorned with human skin—sheets, masks, and clothing all crafted from human flesh. There were human skulls used as bowls and lampshades, and the remains of several women scattered across the house. In the shed outside, the officers found the body of a woman, her body entirely skinned, her remains arranged in a grotesque fashion as if she were a doll. Among the many unsettling discoveries were two complete human faces hanging on hooks, the eyes of the victims staring vacantly into the void.

One of the most disturbing revelations was the collection of "body parts" scattered throughout the house. There were piles of body parts—hands, feet, and organs—carefully preserved in jars. The sheer amount of remains was staggering, yet somehow, Gein had managed to operate with this macabre collection for months, if not years, without attracting any suspicion from the local community. These grotesque objects, kept as if they were trophies, spoke volumes about the depths of Gein's disturbed psyche.

The officers were not only stunned by what they found, but they were also gripped by an intense disbelief. How could someone so seemingly ordinary have been hiding such depravity in plain sight? Ed Gein was a man who had lived alone in that farmhouse for years, never married, and barely interacted with the townsfolk. His reclusive nature and odd mannerisms had been dismissed as eccentricities, but the horrifying truth that lay behind his closed doors shattered the calm facade of Plainfield.

The immediate reaction from law enforcement was one of shock, followed by a sense of disbelief that the human mind could descend into such darkness. For the first time, the small town of Plainfield realized that the man they had all seen walking around town, the man who was known to be quiet and seemingly harmless, was responsible for unimaginable horrors.

Many of the officers involved in the investigation later admitted that they would never forget the horrors they had witnessed that day. One officer even stated that upon seeing the bodies, he thought the entire situation felt like a nightmare. Yet it was all too real.

The police had no idea how long Gein had been committing these murders. The gruesome evidence was overwhelming, yet the most unsettling fact was that he had apparently carried out these crimes in complete isolation, without the knowledge of the outside world. His entire life had been built around his mother, Augusta, whose death had led him further down the path of madness. Her deeply religious and oppressive influence had shaped Gein's warped view of the world, and after her passing, he had sought to create his own "family" of sorts—through human remains.

At first, the authorities were unsure of how many victims Gein had claimed. The discovery of the human remains, including organs and body parts, hinted at a larger scale of violence. After all, the house was filled with items constructed from body parts. There were reports of human bones fashioned into utensils, chairs made of human skin, and even a human skull being used as a drinking vessel. These trophies were not just evidence of murder but seemed to reveal a sadistic need to create a twisted home life for himself, with the human remains as his twisted companions.

The investigation quickly turned into a nationwide spectacle, with news outlets reporting every grisly detail. The press descended on Plainfield, where rumors spread about the horrific nature of Gein's actions. The term "serial killer" was not widely used at the time, but it would soon be applied to Gein. He had become a household name, a name that would forever be associated with the most depraved form of human behavior.

As authorities continued their investigation, the town of Plainfield was gripped with a strange mixture of fear, disgust, and fascination. Many of the locals, having known Ed Gein as a quiet and eccentric figure, were unable to reconcile the man they thought they knew with the monster they now realized he had become. People who had passed him on the street, waved to him in the local diner, and exchanged pleasantries with him were now forced to come to terms with the knowledge that this unassuming man had been capable of such horrifying acts.

The authorities, while shocked, remained focused on their goal: understanding how and why Ed Gein committed these heinous acts. They began interviewing Gein, trying to piece together the full extent of his crimes. It became clear that Gein was not only disturbed but also deeply delusional. He claimed that he had been inspired by his mother's teachings to create a "female body" to replace her. This bizarre justification for his actions revealed the extent to which Gein's mind had been warped by years of isolation and obsession with his mother.

As the investigation progressed, more details about Gein's actions began to surface. He had exhumed bodies from nearby cemeteries, desecrating graves to acquire fresh corpses that he could use to complete his "collection." He had an eerie fascination with death, and the bodies he exhumed were often used to create his grotesque trophies—furniture made of bone, masks made of skin, and a vast array of bizarre, macabre creations. His attempts to create a twisted world for himself—an alternate reality where he could be close to the women he killed, especially his deceased mother—became more apparent as the investigation continued.

The reactions of the law enforcement officers who entered Gein's home ranged from stunned silence to palpable disgust. Some of them later confessed to having nightmares about the crime scene, while others would never be able to forget the sight of the skin masks and the jars of organs. As the gruesome evidence piled up, it became increasingly clear that Ed Gein had been living in a nightmare of his own creation, and the world would soon understand just how deep that nightmare truly went.

In the end, the discovery at Ed Gein's farmhouse did not just reveal a killer. It uncovered the profound depths of a disturbed mind, twisted by grief, isolation, and an obsessive need for control. His macabre trophies were not merely the result of murder—they were the tragic expression of a man who had lost his way, shaped by a warped vision of love, death, and identity. The horrors inside that farmhouse were a revelation—one that would forever mark Ed Gein as one of the most infamous and disturbing figures in American criminal history.

Chapter Six

Behind the Masks

Ed Gein, a name that will forever be synonymous with grotesque violence and twisted psychological turmoil, became notorious for crimes that went beyond the physical. His obsession with body parts, his crafting of masks, furniture, and clothing from human remains, and his horrifying creation of a "female suit" have shaped him into a symbol of madness in America's criminal history. The unsettling things he did with the human bodies he collected were not simply about the macabre; they represented a complex and deeply disturbing fusion of need, trauma, and identity.

Gein's grotesque hobby began not with murder but with a deep fascination with death and the human body. After his mother's death in 1945, the floodgates of Ed's disturbed psyche opened. His intense need for control over the living and the dead grew exponentially. His obsession with his mother's death and the morbid ways in which he sought to preserve her, both physically and psychologically, became the cornerstone of his eventual crimes. He didn't just take human lives; he dissected them, transformed them, and made them into objects that served his warped needs.

In the early 1950s, reports began to surface of an eccentric local man—an isolated figure who spent long hours in his rural Plainfield farmhouse, where odd noises echoed from his property. Gein had developed an interest in grave robbing, first targeting the recently deceased in the local cemetery. His victims, mostly women, resembled his mother in age and appearance. He would dig up their bodies and bring them back to his home, where he would perform grotesque rituals. Gein's most disturbing creations, however, came from his need to build something that would allow him to feel connected to the woman he could never fully possess—his mother, Augusta Gein.

His "craft" was a grotesque display of a sick imagination. Gein crafted masks and lampshades from human skin, pillows made from body parts, and upholstered furniture using human tissue. These objects served not just as reminders of the dead but as an attempt to give Ed a false sense of control and power over life and death. In a mind that had been twisted by a complex cocktail of trauma, isolation, and unresolved psychosexual issues, these "projects" represented his ultimate quest for possession and transformation.

But perhaps the most chilling of all was the suit Gein crafted for himself—a "female suit" made entirely from human skin, including the face, breasts, and genitalia. Gein's desire to create this macabre suit was not only a reflection of his intense hatred and fear of women, but also an indication of his convoluted ideas about gender, identity, and his own psychological disintegration. By wearing the skin of a woman, Gein seemed to believe he could embody something he had always craved—access to a maternal and feminine identity, without the emotional complexities or limitations imposed by a real woman.

The psychological implications of this act are profound. Gein's distorted view of gender and identity stemmed largely from his turbulent relationship with his mother. Augusta Gein was a deeply religious woman who instilled in Ed a belief in the evils of women and sex. He was told by his mother that women were the source of all sin, and that only through her did he find salvation. Augusta's dominance in his life, combined with her death, left Ed with a chaotic emotional and psychological void. His creation of a female suit can be understood as an attempt to resolve the conflict between his profound desire for maternal love and the overwhelming hatred he harbored toward women.

This fixation on transforming himself into a woman can be seen as an attempt to merge the two opposing forces that shaped Gein's identity—his intense attachment to his mother and his desire to punish her. It was as though by physically becoming a woman, Gein could subjugate his mother's memory and her values. The "female suit" allowed him to embody a figure that was both an object of his obsession and a manifestation of his perverse need for control. It was a form of extreme regression, where the boundary between reality and fantasy dissolved, and Ed's internal chaos was externalized in horrific ways.

Gein's relationship with gender identity was further complicated by his own reclusive, hermetic life. Having been isolated for so long, his understanding of himself and his sexual identity was grossly distorted. The concept of being a man or woman, of gender as we understand it, may have become irrelevant to Ed. His psychological condition, possibly rooted in deep trauma, led him to view himself in a way that merged his desires, fears, and fantasies in a horrific and psychotic synthesis. His creation of female body parts and clothing from the remains of women was an attempt to erase any difference between the two sexes, to become something that didn't exist in the real world. This act transcended simple cross-dressing or gender dysphoria; it was an extreme rejection of societal norms and a complete breakdown of his identity. By becoming a woman through these acts, he may have been seeking a form of rebirth—a new identity, one not bound by the limitations of his former life.

Ed Gein's crafting of human remains into masks and clothing also represents an inversion of the natural order. The dead were brought to life in an artificial form; skin was turned into something other than its intended purpose. The human body, which should have been allowed to rest in peace, became a canvas for Ed's twisted artistic expression. In his mind, he wasn't just collecting parts of the dead; he was creating something that could make him whole. He was attempting to reconstruct himself, piece by piece, from the body parts of those who had been buried—recreating a version of a woman, of a mother, and of himself, using grotesque materials that could never fill the emptiness inside him.

In the years that followed, when authorities discovered the full extent of Gein's crimes, the true horror of his actions was realized. The masks, the furniture, the grotesque items all painted a chilling portrait of a man who had become so detached from reality that he could no longer distinguish between the living and the dead, the real and the imagined. His obsession with creating objects and personas from human remains reflected not just a psychological breakdown but a complete rejection of the human experience. Gein had no longer seen himself or the world around him as anything but raw materials for his own disturbed desires.

What truly sets Ed Gein apart from many of history's most notorious killers is not just the brutality of his crimes, but the psychotic, distorted logic behind them. He was not simply killing and taking lives; he was creating and reassembling a new identity for himself from the remnants of those he killed. His crafting of masks, furniture, and the female suit was a physical manifestation of his attempt to control his fractured identity—a transformation that would never allow him to be truly whole.

Gein's crimes were not just about mutilation; they were a misguided attempt to repair his broken self, to reconcile with his mother, and to embody a distorted version of womanhood. His actions revealed a fractured mind that could not comprehend the boundaries of identity, gender, and morality. By transforming the human body into art, Gein blurred the lines between horror and creation, and in doing so, he became one of the most psychologically complex and terrifying figures in criminal history.

As we delve deeper into the story of Ed Gein, the horror of his crimes becomes even more apparent—not just in the brutality of his acts, but in the twisted psychology that drove him. Gein's need to craft, to create something from death, is a chilling reflection of the ways in which trauma and identity can intersect in the most destructive of ways. The "female suit" was not just a piece of clothing; it was a manifestation of a disturbed mind that sought to find some kind of peace in the most grotesque of ways. And as the world would learn, this suit would forever be a symbol of the monstrosity that Ed Gein became.

Gein's transformation into the monster that captivated the world was not just a matter of crime but a complex psychological descent into darkness. His obsession with body parts and his grotesque crafting of masks and clothing were an attempt to patch together a fractured identity—one that ultimately could not be healed, no matter how hard he tried.

Chapter Seven

The Psychological Profile of Ed Gein

"The world is full of monsters with friendly faces." — Unknown

Ed Gein's story is not one of just horror, but of the disturbing, complex interplay between mental illness, trauma, and violence. His actions were both shocking and deeply rooted in a troubled psychological landscape, one that unfolded within the confines of his isolated childhood home. As we explore the psychological profile of Ed Gein, we must try to understand not only the criminal he became but also the damaged and broken man who suffered in silence for much of his life.

While his crimes have become the stuff of legend, the true horror lies not only in the gruesome nature of his actions but in the mental state that led him to commit them. In Ed's case, understanding the psychological conditions that drove him—schizophrenia, psychosis, and possibly dissociative identity disorder—offers us a glimpse into the depths of human darkness.

Ed Gein was born in 1906 in La Crosse, Wisconsin, into a deeply religious and domineering household. His mother, Augusta, was a fundamentalist Christian who instilled in him a fear of sin and the evil that permeated the world. Augusta raised Ed and his brother Henry with an iron fist, teaching them that women were the root of all evil. At an early age, Ed was isolated from the rest of society, and his social interactions were limited to his mother's strict teachings and the bleak environment of their farm. Ed's father, George Gein, was an alcoholic who failed to provide any meaningful support or affection, leaving Augusta to dominate every aspect of his upbringing. This early life of emotional neglect, compounded by his mother's toxic influence, laid the foundation for the psychological issues that would shape Ed's future.

One of the first things that stands out about Ed's behavior is his intense social isolation. As he grew older, he avoided relationships with women, showing little to no interest in dating or forming connections with others. This isolation wasn't simply a preference; it was a deep-seated response to his traumatic upbringing. His loneliness was palpable. The only relationships Ed had were with his mother and, later, with the corpses of women he would exhume from graveyards. His emotional stuntedness is often linked to the fact that Augusta instilled in him a pathological fear of the opposite sex, cultivating a warped view of women as dangerous and corrupt.

Many experts who have studied Gein's case suggest that he may have suffered from **schizophrenia**. Schizophrenia is a mental disorder that is often characterized by distorted thinking, hallucinations, and delusions. In Ed's case, his deeply rooted obsession with death, body parts, and his mother's role in shaping his worldview suggest that he may have had a distorted perception of reality. He exhibited signs of **paranoid schizophrenia**, particularly in his obsessive thoughts and extreme actions toward his mother's preservation after her death. Ed's belief in his ability to commune with the dead, as well as his tendency to see the bodies he exhumed as "real" women, might be seen as symptoms of **delusional thinking**.

Psychosis, a condition often linked to schizophrenia, may have also played a significant role in Ed's behavior. Psychosis refers to a mental state where a person loses touch with reality, experiencing vivid hallucinations or delusions. Ed's behavior often suggested that he was living in a distorted reality, where his actions were justified by his own internal logic. His use of body parts to fashion his "female suit" and other macabre items was likely an attempt to create an idealized version of a woman—one he could control, and one who would never abandon him. This reflects a delusional belief system that was deeply entangled with his personal trauma, social isolation, and distorted views of gender and sexuality.

Another critical aspect of Ed's psychological profile lies in his **sexual frustrations**. While there is no definitive evidence that Ed ever had any sexual encounters, his fixation on women's bodies and his bizarre sexual fantasies about dressing in women's skin point to deep-seated issues with his own sexual identity. Ed's relationship with his mother, who taught him that women were "evil," left him without a healthy outlet for his sexual energy. It seems that Ed was never able to reconcile his feelings of sexual desire with the strict moral teachings instilled by his mother. As a result, he may have developed **sexual deviancy**, where his desires were diverted into necrophilia—his obsession with dead bodies likely being an attempt to fulfill unmet sexual urges.

Ed Gein's **need for control** was another driving force behind his horrific actions. Throughout his life, Ed was subjected to strict control by his mother, and after her death, he sought to reclaim that control in the only way he knew how—through violence. His manipulation of the bodies of dead women, his obsession with creating human-like figures, and his ultimate desire to become a "woman" himself all point to a profound need for dominance over both life and death. The women Ed murdered and exhumed were not simply victims; they were vessels for his desires, embodying a deep, symbolic act of control.

There is also the possibility that Ed Gein suffered from **dissociative identity disorder (DID)**, a condition often linked to severe trauma and childhood abuse. DID is characterized by the presence of two or more distinct personalities within a person, each with its own unique behaviors and memories. In Ed's case, it's possible that his obsession with his mother and his transformation into a female persona were the result of a fragmented sense of self. By dressing in the skins of women, Ed could have been attempting to inhabit an alternate identity—a female one—so he could escape from the torment of his repressed sexual urges and his desperate need to please his mother. His second "identity" was one that allowed him to exert control over his victims, effectively becoming the woman he had so longed for.

Another important factor that contributed to Ed's downward spiral was **trauma**—a combination of emotional, psychological, and environmental factors that deeply affected his mental state. The trauma he experienced in his early years—living in a home ruled by a domineering, religiously fanatic mother, coupled with the death of his brother Henry—likely had a devastating effect on Ed's mental and emotional well-being. His trauma was compounded by the fact that he was never given the tools to process or express his pain in a healthy way. Instead of seeking help or building meaningful relationships, Ed retreated further into isolation, where his fantasies began to manifest into horrific actions.

Ed Gein's life and behavior suggest a complex interaction of mental illness, trauma, and isolation, which fed into his violent tendencies. His schizophrenia, sexual deviancy, and need for control were all interwoven into the fabric of his being, making him an increasingly dangerous individual. His actions were not those of a rational mind, but of a tortured soul seeking to express, albeit in the most horrifying ways, a deep need for connection, for control, and for release from the constraints of the life he had been forced to live.

As we delve deeper into the mind of Ed Gein, it becomes clear that his psychological profile is not one of a simple, monstrous killer but one of an individual shaped by profound trauma and mental illness. While his crimes cannot be justified, understanding the psychological conditions that led him to commit them may offer some insight into the dark recesses of the human mind. Ed Gein's story serves as a grim reminder that mental illness, when left untreated and unaddressed, can lead to devastating consequences—not only for the person suffering but for those around them.

Chapter Eight

Gein's Gruesome Hobby

The human desire for connection, affection, and the quest for identity often manifests in complex ways, especially for those whose life experiences are shaped by isolation, trauma, and distorted perceptions of the world. Ed Gein, one of the most notorious figures in American criminal history, is an embodiment of this twisted pursuit of identity and belonging. His gruesome hobby of collecting and preserving human body parts was not just a manifestation of his deviance but a twisted form of psychological survival—a desperate attempt to fill the vast emptiness left by his traumatic experiences.

Ed Gein's methods of collecting human remains were horrifying in their simplicity yet deeply unsettling in their execution. He would often rob graves in the nearby cemetery, selecting the bodies of recently deceased women. His obsession with exhuming the dead was fueled not by a desire to terrorize the living but by a deep-seated yearning to "reconnect" with the women who had shaped his life: his domineering mother, Augusta, and the women he fantasized about. These grave robbing excursions were not the sporadic acts of a random killer; they were, in Gein's disturbed mind, a way of forming a relationship with the dead.

The bodies Gein unearthed were meticulously dismembered, their skin and bones stripped of their identity. The methods Gein employed in his macabre "crafting" process were as methodical as they were horrifying. He would carefully peel the skin from the bodies, turning it into leather-like material that he would use to create masks, furniture, and even clothing. His fascination with human skin was not just about the morbid nature of the act, but about the power he believed he could wield by possessing it. He was not just preserving body parts; he was trying to preserve the essence of life—life that had been taken from him at a young age when he lost the love and protection of his mother, Augusta. For Gein, the act of skinning the dead was a grotesque form of reclaiming control over his life.

The psychological and emotional factors behind Gein's collection of body parts can be traced to his deeply fractured psyche. Raised in an environment where his mother instilled in him an overwhelming sense of guilt and shame, Gein was led to view women through a lens of both admiration and fear. Augusta Gein, a fanatical religious woman, taught Ed that all women were evil, lustful creatures who would ultimately lead him to damnation. At the same time, she was the only woman in Ed's life, a woman who demanded complete devotion and whose power over him shaped the entirety of his existence. After Augusta's death, Ed's repressed desires, mixed with his profound loneliness, caused him to spiral into violent acts of desperation.

Gein's obsession with preserving human skin and body parts can be viewed through the lens of his need for a maternal figure. The creation of his "female suit," one of the most grotesque and symbolic artifacts of his crimes, encapsulates his complex psychological needs. The suit, made from the skin of women, was a twisted attempt by Ed to resurrect his mother. This act was not simply about fashioning a macabre garment—it was about reimagining his own identity through a female body. By wearing the suit, Gein sought to experience womanhood in the most literal way possible. He did not merely wish to dress as a woman; he desired to fully embody a woman's role, to feel what it was like to possess a maternal, nurturing identity—something he had been denied in his life.

The female suit was, in many ways, Gein's attempt to merge with the very figure who had controlled and dominated his life. It represented a grotesque form of identification with the mother he had so deeply internalized. Wearing it allowed him to feel closer to her, as if by wearing the skin of another woman, he could recapture the lost affection, approval, and power he had once craved from Augusta. The act of donning the suit was deeply sexualized, a way for Gein to express his repressed sexual urges while maintaining control over them. By stripping the women of their identities, Gein was able to possess them in a way that allowed him to suppress his fears of rejection and abandonment.

But there was more to his need for the suit than just maternal longing. The suit also reflected Gein's intense sexual frustration and inability to form healthy relationships with living women. His social ineptitude, combined with his distorted view of women, meant that he never learned how to navigate intimacy in a way that was emotionally fulfilling. In his mind, the women he had killed and skinned became nothing more than objects of possession, tools for him to manipulate and control. The creation of the suit was a grotesque expression of this power—an attempt to sublimate his desires into a tangible object that he could mold, touch, and feel in a way that bypassed the need for human interaction.

Gein's actions were not just the product of a disturbed mind; they were the result of an intense emotional need for intimacy and connection. His obsession with collecting and preserving body parts was an attempt to find a sense of control and ownership over his life. The bodies of the women he exhumed or murdered became blank slates onto which Gein projected his fantasies and frustrations. The skins he peeled away represented the walls he had built around his emotions, a way of distancing himself from the reality of his loneliness and despair.

His obsession with human skin and the creation of the female suit also symbolized the deeper need for an identity. Gein had spent most of his life in a shadow, a figure defined by his overbearing mother and his own self-loathing. By creating these suits and masks, he was trying to carve out a sense of self that had eluded him for so long. The female persona he created was the only identity he could fully inhabit, a distorted form of femininity that allowed him to feel powerful and yet deeply disconnected from reality. It was a grotesque form of self-expression, one that distorted his internal sense of self in an attempt to create a reality where he could find peace, if only for a fleeting moment.

The twisted nature of Gein's actions is a chilling reminder of how the human need for connection and belonging can become warped when guided by trauma and isolation. His collection of body parts was not just an act of violence; it was an attempt to control, preserve, and redefine his world. It was about attempting to fill the gaping void left by his mother's death, by the isolation he had lived in, and by the deep-seated emotional scars that had never been addressed. In his mind, these body parts, these women, represented something that he had lost and could never truly replace. They were his last desperate attempt to recreate a world where he could find both a sense of power and the love he had never truly known.

Gein's "female suit" and his obsession with human skin stand as grotesque symbols of the psychological scars that shaped his entire existence. They are a testament to how a disturbed mind can distort the most basic human needs—love, identity, and intimacy—into horrific expressions of violence and possession. What drove Ed Gein to create these macabre relics was not simply a need for sexual release or control, but a deep, twisted longing to fill the emptiness inside him with something that could never truly satisfy. His creations were a reflection of his desperation, his inability to relate to others, and his warped attempt to find himself in the lives of the women he killed and desecrated.

The tragedy of Ed Gein lies not only in the horrors he committed but in the psychological and emotional voids that drove him to those acts. His gruesome hobby was a manifestation of his distorted understanding of identity, a reflection of a man who, in his isolation, lost all sense of humanity and instead clung to an identity formed by the most perverse of means.

Chapter Nine

The Police Investigation

In the winter of 1957, as the tiny rural community of Plainfield, Wisconsin, braced against the cold, the horrifying truth about the quiet, reclusive Ed Gein was about to be unearthed. Gein, a man whose bizarre and unsettling behavior had long been an enigma to neighbors and acquaintances, was about to become the central figure in one of the most grotesque investigations in criminal history. The events that led to his arrest would not only shake a small town to its core but also send ripples through American society that continue to reverberate in the realms of criminology, popular culture, and the human psyche.

The breakthrough in the investigation began with the disappearance of a local hardware store owner named Bernice Worden. On November 16, 1957, Worden vanished without a trace from her business, leaving behind a scene that hinted at foul play. Her son, Frank Worden, a deputy sheriff, was immediately concerned. He knew his mother well enough to suspect that something sinister had happened. The day after her disappearance, Frank noticed that her truck had gone missing, and her cash register was gone too. This was no ordinary theft. It was a chilling sign that something far darker had taken place.

Worden's disappearance was not the first in the area. Only days earlier, local authorities had been investigating the disappearance of another woman, a young tavern owner named Mary Hogan. Hogan had vanished without a trace in 1954, leaving her home and business abandoned. At the time, there had been no leads, and the case had gone cold. But now, with Worden's disappearance, the town was on edge. The sudden and unexplained vanishing of two women in such a small town seemed too much to be mere coincidence. The authorities were under increasing pressure to find answers.

The initial investigation into Worden's disappearance seemed to lead nowhere. Sheriff Art Schley and his team questioned neighbors, friends, and family, but they had little to go on. As the days dragged on with no clues, the pressure mounted. Yet, the breakthrough came unexpectedly when Frank Worden recalled a peculiar detail. He had recently learned that his mother's vanishing coincided with a visit to Gein's farm. This connection, though slight, was the key to the case's unraveling.

Gein had been known to authorities in the past. He had a long-standing reputation in the community as an eccentric recluse. He had never been fully trusted, but his oddities had never raised enough suspicion for law enforcement to investigate him seriously. But now, with the suspicion that he had been involved in Worden's disappearance, the police had to confront the disturbing possibility that the quiet, seemingly harmless Gein was hiding something far darker beneath the surface.

Sheriff Schley and his team made the decision to pay a visit to Gein's farmhouse, located just outside Plainfield. The house was as peculiar as its owner. It stood alone at the edge of the small farming town, shrouded in an eerie, unsettling quiet. Gein had always kept to himself, and his farm was known for its dilapidated state. It was the kind of place that locals didn't visit unless absolutely necessary. Yet, no one could have predicted what the officers would find when they arrived.

The investigation began at the barn on Gein's property. Gein himself was initially cooperative, but his strange demeanor raised red flags. As Schley and his team entered the barn, the first disturbing sign came when they discovered a bloodstained rifle hanging from the wall. Yet, it was what they found next that would cement Gein's role in the murders. In a small room behind the barn, the officers discovered the dismembered body of Bernice Worden. Her body had been mutilated beyond recognition, gutted like an animal and hung from a chain, as though she were a carcass waiting to be butchered. This macabre display sent a chill through the investigators. The realization that Gein was connected to Worden's murder became undeniable.

But the true horror would unfold once the police began to search Gein's house. Inside, they discovered a scene more disturbing than anyone could have imagined. Gein had transformed his home into a twisted shrine of human remains.

Among the items found were human skin masks, a lampshade made from human skin, and furniture crafted from bones and skulls. It became apparent that Gein had been using body parts for his grotesque crafts. But the extent of his obsession was not fully understood at this point. What shocked the investigators even further was the realization that these were not just pieces of random body parts. The evidence suggested that Gein had been collecting the remains of women, specifically targeting women who resembled his deceased mother. The psychological profile began to take shape.

The more the investigators delved into Gein's past, the more bizarre and disturbing details came to light. They learned that Gein had been obsessed with death and the human body for years. His fascination with corpses began in the late 1940s, shortly after his mother's death. He would visit graveyards, exhuming bodies of women who resembled his mother, and bring them back to his farm to use as his twisted mannequins. The discoveries in his home confirmed that Gein had been living in a nightmarish world of his own creation, re-enacting fantasies of motherhood and sexuality. His actions were not those of a rational mind, but rather the work of a deeply disturbed individual consumed by a warped need for control.

While the discovery of Bernice Worden's body and the collection of human remains shocked the public, the investigation was far from over. Authorities now faced the daunting task of unraveling the full scope of Gein's crimes. How many victims had there been? How many women had been lured to his farm under the guise of a harmless man who lived alone? Gein's arrest brought a sense of relief to the small town, but it also left a gaping hole of fear and unease that would never truly be filled.

One of the most difficult challenges faced by investigators was piecing together the exact timeline of Gein's crimes. His erratic behavior and inconsistent confessions made it hard to trust his statements. At times, Gein would admit to the murders of several women, but at other times, he would deny it, claiming he was only guilty of grave robbing. His unreliable memory and shifting narratives made it impossible to fully reconstruct his actions. The lack of hard evidence and the lack of witnesses to any of the murders only complicated matters further.

However, as the investigation progressed, additional clues and breakthroughs began to emerge. Law enforcement officers, working closely with forensic experts and psychologists, began to understand Gein's disturbing psychology. They pieced together his actions through his own twisted confessions, forensic evidence from his farm, and interviews with those who had known him. Over time, they confirmed that Gein had been responsible for the murders of at least two women—Mary Hogan and Bernice Worden—but he was also suspected of other disappearances dating back years. The realization that the full extent of his crimes might never be known haunted the investigators, leaving the question of how many victims Gein might have claimed unanswered.

Despite the bizarre and terrifying nature of the case, the investigation was ultimately considered a success. The arrest of Ed Gein marked the end of a chilling chapter in Wisconsin's history, but it also raised unsettling questions about the nature of evil and the hidden darkness that can reside in even the most ordinary of places. Gein's arrest and the revelations that followed would serve as a cautionary tale about the fragility of the human mind and the horrors that can emerge from the depths of a disturbed psyche.

The case of Ed Gein was one that defied logic and reason, and the investigation into his crimes was fraught with challenges. Yet, through persistence, meticulous detective work, and the uncovering of key evidence, law enforcement was able to bring a killer to justice. But even as the case closed, the nightmare lingered, and the name Ed Gein would forever be linked to one of the most disturbing criminal investigations in history.

Chapter Ten

The Trial of Ed Gein

The courtroom was a stage for one of the most chilling and macabre trials in American criminal history, a trial that captivated the nation, repulsed the public, and sparked debates on the intersection of mental illness and criminal responsibility. When Ed Gein stood before a judge in 1957, the eyes of America were fixed on the small town of Plainfield, Wisconsin, where the line between horror and reality had been irrevocably blurred. The case was a spectacle that would not only change the course of criminal law but also shape the way society views the relationship between madness and murder.

Ed Gein had been arrested in November 1957 after the gruesome discovery of body parts, including human skin, skulls, and other body parts, in his home. What began as the investigation of a missing woman, Bernice Worden, quickly spiraled into a horrific revelation of Gein's disturbing crimes. As investigators unearthed the horrifying details of his activities, it became clear that Gein had not only murdered two women but had also exhumed corpses from local graveyards, creating a grotesque collection of body parts with which he crafted masks, furniture, and even a suit made of human skin. The case stunned the nation, but the true drama was yet to unfold in the courtroom.

The trial began in the spring of 1968, over a decade after Gein's arrest, and it was, by all accounts, a spectacle of the highest order. The small town of Plainfield had been thrust into the national spotlight, and the world watched as the details of Gein's atrocities were revealed. The courtroom was crowded, with curious spectators and media outlets eager to witness the trial of the man who had become a living legend of terror. Journalists from across the country flocked to the courthouse, filing stories that would later cement Ed Gein's place in the annals of criminal infamy.

The trial itself, however, was not a straightforward criminal case. Ed Gein was not a man who had simply committed a crime out of malice or greed. The prosecution's case had to navigate a deeply unsettling question: was Ed Gein, the man who had created a female suit from human skin, mentally competent to stand trial? This question was at the core of the proceedings. Gein's defense team, led by defense attorney Fredrick J. Gray, would argue that their client was not responsible for his actions because he was suffering from severe mental illness. The prosecution, on the other hand, had a much more difficult task. They needed to prove that Gein's actions were driven not by insanity but by malice, and that he should be held accountable for the two murders he was charged with.

The prosecution's strategy was to show the court that Gein was fully aware of his actions and the consequences of those actions. They attempted to portray him as a man driven by perverse desires, someone who acted with a level of intent that defied the boundaries of insanity. To bolster their argument, the prosecution presented the chilling evidence found in Gein's home: the skulls and masks, the female suit made from human skin, and the grisly tools he used to dismember and preserve his victims. These were not the actions of a man who had lost touch with reality, the prosecution argued. Instead, they depicted him as a man who had used his knowledge of the human body for his own dark purposes, a man who had methodically crafted his gruesome collection with clear and calculated intent.

However, the defense countered with a compelling argument of their own. They argued that Ed Gein was a deeply disturbed individual, suffering from a combination of schizophrenia and obsessive-compulsive disorder. His obsession with his deceased mother, Augusta Gein, and his distorted views on sexuality and gender were central to the defense's case. The defense called on psychiatric experts who testified that Ed Gein had been so consumed by his psychosis that he could not have fully understood the nature of his crimes. They argued that his mental illness had clouded his ability to differentiate between right and wrong, and as such, he was incapable of standing trial in a conventional sense.

The prosecution, realizing the difficulty of proving that Gein had acted with full awareness, shifted their strategy toward proving that his crimes were driven by an undeniable pathology, not mere insanity. They called on witnesses, including law enforcement officers who had investigated the case, to describe the grisly scene they encountered when they entered Gein's home. The images of the human skin masks, the decayed remains of the bodies, and the grotesque rituals Gein had performed were meant to shock the jury into seeing Gein as a monster—someone who had knowingly embraced his horrific urges rather than succumbed to a mental illness that rendered him incapable of understanding his actions.

As the trial continued, the psychiatric evaluations of Ed Gein became a central issue. Several experts were brought in to assess Gein's mental state. Dr. Joseph D. O'Keefe, a psychiatrist who examined Gein, testified that the defendant was suffering from "severe mental illness," which included a significant amount of schizophrenia. He explained that Gein's obsession with his mother had led him to commit his crimes as a form of psychological regression, as if he were trying to "bring her back" in some twisted way. This explanation of Gein's psychosis, though chilling, painted a picture of a man who was, in the defense's view, incapable of distinguishing between fantasy and reality.

Dr. O'Keefe's testimony helped to solidify the defense's case, and Gein's plea of not guilty by reason of insanity was eventually accepted. The court declared that Gein was not fit to stand trial for murder, and he was found not guilty by reason of insanity. He was committed to the Central State Hospital for the Criminally Insane in Waupun, Wisconsin, where he would spend the remainder of his life.

The verdict was a bittersweet resolution to the trial. On one hand, it meant that Gein would not face the death penalty or life in prison for his crimes. On the other hand, it underscored the complexity of the relationship between mental illness and criminal responsibility. While some saw the verdict as a victory for justice, others viewed it as a failure to properly hold Gein accountable for the suffering he had caused. The decision sparked heated debates in legal circles and among the public, with many questioning whether it was possible to ever truly understand the mind of a killer like Ed Gein.

In the years following the trial, Ed Gein became a symbol of the darker side of human nature, an example of how the boundaries between madness and malice can be disturbingly thin.

His story would inspire countless books, films, and documentaries, all of which sought to understand how a man could descend into such madness. Some portrayed him as a tragic figure, a victim of his own mental illness, while others saw him as a monster—a man who chose to embrace his depravity.

The psychological evaluations that played a crucial role in the trial continue to influence the study of criminal psychology today. Gein's case forced legal professionals and mental health experts to grapple with the difficult question of how to hold individuals accountable for their actions when they are clearly suffering from severe mental illness. In the end, Gein's trial did not offer any simple answers, but it did set a precedent for future cases involving the intersection of mental health and criminal law.

The trial of Ed Gein was not just about a man who had committed horrific murders. It was a trial that exposed the complexities of the human mind and the moral and legal dilemmas that arise when society must decide how to treat individuals who are both victims and perpetrators of their own twisted realities.

Chapter Eleven

The Aftermath and Cultural Impact

"When the mind is tortured by the weight of its own thoughts, the most grotesque realities seem like salvation."

In the late 1950s, the world was introduced to a man who would forever change the way we think about horror, crime, and the darker recesses of the human psyche. Ed Gein, a simple man from Plainfield, Wisconsin, became the center of one of the most shocking and macabre investigations in American history. His crimes were as bizarre as they were horrifying, and his arrest in 1957 ignited a media frenzy that both captivated and repulsed the public.

The media's response to Ed Gein's crimes was not just about the facts of his brutal acts. It was the grotesque spectacle of his crimes, the ghastly objects found in his home, and the revelation of his twisted psychological state that made headlines for weeks, months, and even years. In the days leading up to his arrest, the townspeople of Plainfield were blissfully unaware of the horrors lurking in their midst. Gein's peculiar habits and solitary lifestyle had always been a subject of gossip, but no one suspected the full extent of his deranged tendencies. When authorities uncovered his disturbing collection of human remains—skin, bones, and even masks—America was shocked, appalled, and transfixed.

The media quickly descended on Plainfield, and Ed Gein became the face of evil in America. News outlets from across the country flooded the small town, seeking details of the grisly discovery and attempting to uncover the psychology behind such brutal acts. The story of the reclusive man who had transformed his house into a macabre chamber of horrors filled newspapers, magazines, and television broadcasts. Gein's trial and subsequent confinement to a mental institution became one of the most sensationalized court cases of the time, capturing the imagination of the public.

For many Americans, the trial was more than just a legal proceeding—it was a window into a twisted world that was both unfathomable and mesmerizing. Reporters lined the courtroom, eager to capture every detail, from the chilling accounts of Gein's crimes to the psychological analyses that revealed the depth of his insanity. The fact that Gein had led a quiet, almost reclusive life in a small, rural town made his crimes all the more shocking. In contrast to the sensational nature of his actions, Gein was portrayed as a seemingly normal man who had descended into madness, making it difficult for the public to reconcile his outward appearance with the gruesome reality of his actions.

The widespread media coverage of Gein's trial not only fed the public's fascination with the case but also fueled a cultural obsession with the psychology of killers. The media presented Ed Gein as both a monster and a tragic figure, a man whose psychological trauma and intense relationship with his domineering mother had shaped his descent into depravity. The public's insatiable appetite for details about his crimes led to the creation of an entire genre of "true crime" reporting that continues to thrive today.

This obsession with Gein extended beyond the trial, spilling into other facets of American culture. Gein's story would go on to influence the development of the modern horror genre, particularly in films and literature. He became an archetype for a new kind of villain, one whose horrific acts were not born of supernatural forces, but of deeply disturbed, human impulses. His crimes touched on some of society's greatest fears—the loss of identity, the breakdown of family structures, and the darkness that can reside in the minds of seemingly ordinary people.

The character of Norman Bates in Robert Bloch's 1959 novel *Psycho* was one of the earliest and most obvious literary creations inspired by Ed Gein. Bates, like Gein, lived a quiet, isolated life with his domineering mother, and his split personality led him to commit gruesome murders. Gein's influence on Bates is clear: both characters are tormented by the memory of their mothers, and both indulge in a warped form of identity creation through violence. In the 1960 Alfred Hitchcock film adaptation of *Psycho*, the character of Bates was solidified as one of the most memorable and terrifying figures in cinematic history. The image of Bates, with his mother's voice echoing in his mind, would go on to inspire generations of filmmakers and writers, cementing Gein's place in the pantheon of cultural villains.

Gein's influence can also be seen in Tobe Hooper's 1974 horror classic *The Texas Chainsaw Massacre*. The character of Leatherface, with his grotesque mask made from human skin, is a direct homage to Gein's morbid habit of using human body parts to create his personal trophies. The idea of Leatherface as a man living in isolation, driven to madness by his family's dysfunction, mirrors Gein's own descent into insanity. Like Gein, Leatherface's horrific acts are not merely the result of evil intentions but are shaped by his upbringing and psychological trauma. *The Texas Chainsaw Massacre* would go on to become one of the most influential films in the slasher genre, and Leatherface remains an enduring symbol of Gein's cultural legacy.

Perhaps one of the most enduring characters inspired by Gein is Buffalo Bill, the villain in Thomas Harris's 1988 novel *The Silence of the Lambs*, and its 1991 film adaptation. Buffalo Bill, whose desire to skin women and create a "suit" for himself echoes Gein's disturbing collection of body parts, became an iconic figure in the world of psychological thrillers. Like Gein, Buffalo Bill's obsession with gender identity and his use of human remains as a means of creating a new persona is central to his character. The chillingly realistic portrayal of Buffalo Bill in the film, played by Ted Levine, is a testament to the lasting influence of Gein's crimes on popular culture.

While these characters may be fictional, they represent a psychological reality that is deeply rooted in the real-life horrors of Ed Gein. His crimes, and the subsequent media coverage, shaped the way American society viewed serial killers and the psychological motivations behind their actions. The public's fascination with Gein was not merely about his horrific crimes; it was also about understanding the mind of a killer, and the unsettling idea that anyone—no matter how ordinary they seemed—could harbor such monstrous thoughts.

Gein's influence also extended to the field of criminology, where his case became a subject of intense study. His ability to deceive those around him, to hide his true nature in plain sight, contributed to the growing interest in the psychology of serial killers. Researchers and psychologists began to look at Gein's upbringing, his relationship with his mother, and his isolated existence as key factors in understanding the motivations of killers. Gein's case became a blueprint for examining the intersection of mental illness, childhood trauma, and violent crime, and his legacy continues to influence criminal profiling and investigations to this day.

The lasting impact of Ed Gein on popular culture and society at large cannot be overstated. His crimes not only terrified a generation of Americans but also contributed to the creation of a cultural narrative about the nature of evil and the horrors that can lurk in the most unexpected places. Through films, books, and media coverage, Gein's story has lived on, not just as a cautionary tale about the dangers of isolation and mental illness, but as a symbol of the darkness that resides within the human psyche. Even decades after his arrest, Ed Gein remains a figure of both fascination and fear, a reminder that true monstrosity can be found not only in the supernatural but in the twisted depths of the human mind.

Chapter Twelve

The Legacy of a Monster

In the quiet town of Plainfield, Wisconsin, the name Ed Gein still echoes through the corridors of history, not as a figure of mystery but as a chilling reminder of the darkest corners of human nature. Gein, a man whose crimes shocked the world in the 1950s, continues to be a figure of morbid fascination, not only because of the grisly nature of his deeds but also due to the psychological complexity of his mind. The gruesome details of his actions, the macabre trophies he created, and the horrifying reality that he was capable of such horrors, have kept his story alive in the public consciousness for over half a century.

Why does the story of Ed Gein continue to captivate the masses today? The answer lies in the intersection of fear, fascination, and a deep-seated need to understand the nature of evil. The act of looking into the abyss of a man like Gein invites an uncomfortable reflection: if such atrocities could be committed by someone like him, someone so seemingly ordinary, what does that say about the potential for darkness in all of us? There is an undeniable human instinct to confront the grotesque, to peer into the darkest aspects of human behavior and to try and make sense of it.

Gein's life, his psychological descent, and the horrors that followed, are inexorably tied to the question of what makes a monster. People are drawn to such figures because they represent the unknowable, the hidden, and the taboo. Ed Gein wasn't just a killer; he was a man who transformed his deepest fears, repressed desires, and warped sense of reality into something tangible, something grotesque. The images of his crimes — masks made from human skin, furniture fashioned from body parts — are not just acts of violence, but of profound psychological distortion. What Gein did with human remains was a form of possession, a perverse attempt at control and transformation. It is a chilling representation of how trauma and mental illness can warp the mind, leading to a disconnection from reality so severe that it becomes possible to dehumanize others to the point of turning them into objects.

The allure of Gein's story, in part, is the need to reconcile his actions with the fact that he was, for many years, a part of society. He was not some faceless figure from the shadows, but a quiet, odd man from a small town, working as a handyman and living in a decaying farmhouse on the outskirts of Plainfield. The fact that such horrors could come from someone so seemingly innocuous challenges our understanding of evil.

In the case of Gein, we see a grotesque blend of pathology, loneliness, and trauma that leads to the unimaginable. It forces us to ask uncomfortable questions about human nature, about how ordinary individuals, when pushed to their breaking point, can become capable of horrific acts.

In the years following his arrest, Ed Gein became an archetype of the disturbed, solitary killer. His crimes, though horrific, were not singular in nature; they were emblematic of a larger pattern that could be found in other infamous figures in history. Gein's life is frequently compared to that of other notorious criminals like Ted Bundy and Jeffrey Dahmer, and his story is often used as a way to understand the psychology of serial killers. While there have been countless analyses of his mental state, one thing is clear: Gein represents the blurred line between the "normal" and the "monstrous." His crimes were not merely the result of momentary lapses in judgment, but rather the manifestation of years of twisted thinking, isolation, and a warped relationship with his domineering mother, Augusta.

One of the most unsettling aspects of Gein's legacy is the influence his story has had on modern pop culture. The character of Norman Bates from *Psycho*, the chainsaw-wielding Leatherface from *The Texas Chainsaw Massacre*, and even the cannibalistic Buffalo Bill from *The Silence of the Lambs* were all inspired by Gein in one form or another. These characters have become symbols of evil in modern horror, and their continuing presence in film, television, and literature speaks to the enduring cultural fascination with Gein's story. In a way, Ed Gein's monstrosity has been immortalized, packaged, and sold as entertainment, yet at its core, there remains a dark, chilling reminder of the true terror that inspired these fictional figures.

While pop culture has commodified the image of Ed Gein, his true legacy is far more complex. In examining his crimes, we learn not just about one man's descent into madness, but about the vulnerabilities of the human psyche. Gein's story is one of profound loneliness, a product of neglect, a lack of emotional support, and a distorted upbringing under the influence of a deeply religious and controlling mother. His actions were, in part, an attempt to gain control over a life that had been defined by abuse, isolation, and a twisted attachment to his mother's authority. The fact that he created human masks and body part trophies was a grotesque form of defiance, a dark rebellion against a world that had rejected him. His need for transformation and control led him to an identity that was part woman, part monster —

an identity he constructed with the very flesh of his victims.

The psychological lessons drawn from Gein's story are invaluable in understanding the complex nature of evil. His descent into criminality wasn't the result of a single event or trauma, but the culmination of years of mental instability, societal alienation, and the inability to reconcile his inner world with reality. What Gein's life reveals is that evil does not always emerge from a clear-cut path of malice. Instead, it can arise from an inability to process or express emotional pain, from the isolation of a person who has never learned how to relate to others, and from the unchecked development of unhealthy, distorted thoughts. In some ways, Gein's story is a warning about the dangers of neglecting the psychological health of individuals, especially those who appear to be living on the fringes of society.

Gein's story also forces society to confront uncomfortable truths about the role of mental illness in violent crime. While his behavior was undoubtedly influenced by a profound psychological disturbance, the conditions that allowed his atrocities to go unnoticed for so long were systemic. The community of Plainfield failed to recognize the signs of Gein's deteriorating mental state, and in doing so, they allowed him to hide in plain sight. The fear of confronting uncomfortable truths, whether about a neighbor, a family member, or a member of society, allows for the conditions that produce such monsters to persist. In many ways, the failure to recognize the warning signs in Gein's case mirrors how society continues to grapple with issues of mental illness, violence, and the stigma surrounding both.

When reflecting on figures like Ed Gein, society faces the difficult task of remembering them in ways that are both respectful and educational, without glorifying their actions. Gein is not simply a monster, but a reflection of the complexities of the human psyche — the result of years of trauma, psychological dysfunction, and societal failure. His story is a mirror held up to the darkest aspects of the human condition, forcing us to reckon with what lies behind the façade of normalcy that we so often take for granted.

The legacy of Ed Gein is one that endures because it forces us to face uncomfortable truths. His story, rooted in psychological horror, transcends the grotesque details of his crimes and serves as a stark reminder of how fragile the human mind can be. Ed Gein's crimes were not just an anomaly in the annals of American crime history; they are a chilling example of what can happen when the mind, unchecked and unexamined, turns inward and spirals into madness. It is a story that endures because it challenges our understanding of what it means to be human and, in doing so, forces us to question the true nature of evil.